Go Back to Where You Are

by David Greenspan

A Samuel French Acting Edition

SAMUELFRENCH.COM

Copyright © 2013 by David Greenspan

ALL RIGHTS RESERVED

CAUTION: Professionals and amateurs are hereby warned that *GO BACK TO WHERE YOU ARE* is subject to a licensing fee. It is fully protected under the copyright laws of the United States of America, the British Commonwealth, including Canada, and all other countries of the Copyright Union. All rights, including professional, amateur, motion picture, recitation, lecturing, public reading, radio broadcasting, television and the rights of translation into foreign languages are strictly reserved. In its present form the play is dedicated to the reading public only.

The amateur and professional live stage performance rights to *GO BACK TO WHERE YOU ARE* are controlled exclusively by Samuel French, Inc., and licensing arrangements and performance licenses must be secured well in advance of presentation. PLEASE NOTE that amateur licensing fees are set upon application in accordance with your producing circumstances. When applying for a licensing quotation and a performance license please give us the number of performances intended, dates of production, your seating capacity and admission fee. Licensing fees are payable one week before the opening performance of the play to Samuel French, Inc., at 45 W. 25th Street, New York, NY 10010.

Licensing fee of the required amount must be paid whether the play is presented for charity or gain and whether or not admission is charged.

Professional/Stock licensing fees quoted upon application to Samuel French, Inc.

For all other rights than those stipulated above, apply to: Judy Boals, Inc. 307 West 38th street, #812, New York, NY 10018.

Particular emphasis is laid on the question of amateur or professional readings, permission and terms for which must be secured in writing from Samuel French, Inc.

Copying from this book in whole or in part is strictly forbidden by law, and the right of performance is not transferable.

Whenever the play is produced the following notice must appear on all programs, printing and advertising for the play: "Produced by special arrangement with Samuel French, Inc."

Due authorship credit must be given on all programs, printing and advertising for the play.

ISBN 978-0-573-70069-9 Printed in U.S.A. #20435

No one shall commit or authorize any act or omission by which the copyright of, or the right to copyright, this play may be impaired.

No one shall make any changes in this play for the purpose of production.

Publication of this play does not imply availability for performance. Both amateurs and professionals considering a production are strongly advised in their own interests to apply to Samuel French, Inc., for written permission before starting rehearsals, advertising, or booking a theatre.

No part of this book may be reproduced, stored in a retrieval system, or transmitted in any form, by any means, now known or yet to be invented, including mechanical, electronic, photocopying, recording, videotaping, or otherwise, without the prior written permission of the publisher.

MUSIC USE NOTE

Licensees are solely responsible for obtaining formal written permission from copyright owners to use copyrighted music in the performance of this play and are strongly cautioned to do so. If no such permission is obtained by the licensee, then the licensee must use only original music that the licensee owns and controls. Licensees are solely responsible and liable for all music clearances and shall indemnify the copyright owners of the play and their licensing agent, Samuel French, Inc., against any costs, expenses, losses and liabilities arising from the use of music by licensees.

IMPORTANT BILLING AND CREDIT REQUIREMENTS

All producers of *GO BACK TO WHERE YOU ARE* must give credit to the Author of the Play in all programs distributed in connection with performances of the Play, and in all instances in which the title of the Play appears for the purposes of advertising, publicizing or otherwise exploiting the Play and/or a production. The name of the Author *must* appear on a separate line on which no other name appears, immediately following the title and *must* appear in size of type not less than fifty percent of the size of the title type.

In addition the following credit *must* be given in all programs and publicity information distributed in association with this piece:

Playwrights Horizons, Inc., produced the World Premiere of
***Go Back to Where You Are* Off Broadway in 2011**

GO BACK TO WHERE YOU ARE was first produced by Playwrights Horizons at the Peter Jay Sharp Theatre in New York, New York on March 24, 2011. The Director was Leigh Silverman, with sets by Rachel Hauck, costumes by Theresa Squire, and lighting by Matt Frey. The Stage Manager was Kyle Gates. The cast was as follows:

BERNARD	Brian Hutchison
PASSALUS	David Greenspan
CLAIRE	Lisa Banes
CHARLOTTE	Mariann Mayberry
TOM	Stephen Bogardus
WALLY	Michael Izquierdo
MALCOLM/GOD	Tim Hopper

The author wishes to thank Mary Shultz who played the role of Charlotte in previews but left the production due to a family crisis.

CHARACTERS

BERNARD – a playwright

PASSALUS – an actor, demon, assumes the character of Constance Simmons

GOD

CLAIRE – an actress, Bernard's sister

CHARLOTTE – an actress, Claire's friend

TOM – a director, Claire's friend

WALLY – a director, Claire's son

MALCOLM – a set designer, Tom's partner

SETTING

The east end of Long Island, Summer.

AUTHOR'S NOTES

Set minimal – perhaps a few bentwood chairs. No sound effects.

The actor playing Malcolm doubles as God.

All characters remain onstage upon Passalus' second entrance into the play. All but Passalus, Bernard, Malcolm (as God), and Claire exit after Passalus says "And the graves are op'd." When Malcolm and Claire are finished they exit, leaving only Passalus and Bernard.

(**BERNARD** *sets down his valise, looks around.*)

BERNARD. I know this place. I should, I've been coming here since I was a child – since the early 60's. It's July. The warm afternoon breeze. The sound of the surf. And this is the small house our parents purchased back then – long before property became so valuable out here. The small house by the sea they left us – my sister and me.

As you can see, it's not an impressive house. An old stucco affair. Nothing compared to the expensive homes you'll find nearby; we're set back a bit from the beach – we don't have an ocean view.

I say we, but really it's just me. My sister sold her share of the house to me years ago and built one of those expensive homes a little further down the shore. It's a very impressive house with private stairs leading from her deck to the beach.

My name is Bernard. I'm one of the characters – obviously – in the play. I'm a playwright. Or at least I tell myself I'm one. Mainly, I teach playwriting.

This is kind of a weird play. I'll show you what I mean.

PASSALUS. Why does the Lord God visit so insignificant a demon as myself?

GOD. You lead with a question. Better had you said simply, I am summoned, I am here.

PASSALUS. But truly, God of all, I am amazed.

GOD. I would speak with you.

PASSALUS. And how horrible is that! Awful to one like me is the light of God here even in the shadows of Hell. I turn my face and yet your voice as much to me a torment. You bring me to nothing. What is it you want from me, God?

BERNARD. What did I tell you, it's a weird play. I hope I didn't give away too much by showing you that. Probably not, you don't know what's going on. That's good. What else?

Oh, here's the train station. That's not important – I shouldn't even have mentioned that. Why do I keep doing that? The only reason is at the end…oh, never mind. I should just let the play begin.

CLAIRE. Mark died a year ago today –

BERNARD. I get a bit nervous at the beginning of a play. It's hard to know where to begin. At least it is for me. And the story I want to tell you and how to tell it – I get…I guess I just want to get things off on the right foot. But –

CLAIRE. Mark died a year ago today –

BERNARD. Never mind.

CLAIRE. On Carolyn's birthday – and her father twenty years before on the same day. Where has time gone? Wally was devastated by Mark's death – though he saw it coming – we all did. Prostate cancer. Terrible in one so young.

CHARLOTTE. It must be hard on Carolyn, the anniversaries of these deaths falling on her birthday.

CLAIRE. Carolyn? No. If she's anything, she's resilient. Unlike her mother. I've never really recovered from Robert's death. Twenty-one years. Not only was he my husband, he was the best director I ever worked with. In some ways, I feel as though I did my best work with him – and that's…well, sad, don't you think – that my best work is twenty years behind me.

CHARLOTTE. Oh, stop it, Claire, you're a brilliant actress – and you know it. Of course, Robert did wonderful things for you, but you've been glorious time and time again since his death.

CLAIRE. You're such a dear, Charlotte. It's almost funny.

CHARLOTTE. Where is Carolyn?

CLAIRE. She and Wally are taking a walk along the beach. She'll put lunch together when they get back.

CHARLOTTE. Good, I'm starving. *(after a brief pause)* It's so nice of you to have me out, Claire. The city is so oppressive right now with the heat. When do you go into rehearsal?

CLAIRE. First week of September – we preview early October. You may remember I once played Nina – that's almost…thirty-five years ago – with Robert, of course.

CHARLOTTE. Of course I remember, we weren't out of school more than a couple of months. You were superb.

CLAIRE. People were so kind.

CHARLOTTE. I tried to get an audition for this production, for Paulina. I did as you suggested, had my agents make a push for it. I suppose they have bigger fish to fry.

CLAIRE. You would have been wonderful. But you're going out to Cleveland to do that wonderful *Annie* musical. I envy you that you sing, I wish I could. You'll have so much fun. You work all the time.

CHARLOTTE. Regionally, yes. I just wish I could get work in town.

CLAIRE. You're an inspiration to me. That reminds me, Tom and Malcolm will be joining us for lunch – I can't believe I forgot to tell you, I hope you don't mind.

CHARLOTTE. Why would I? I adore Tom. I wonder if he remembers me?

CLAIRE. What do you mean, remembers you. Of course he does.

CHARLOTTE. Are you sure? If that's the case, I should have written him myself asking for an audition, instead of just having my agents…Oh, damn! Why didn't I do that? I'm so stupid! That's what I should have done.

CLAIRE. Darling, let it go. It's only a play. One play in a lifetime of plays.

CHARLOTTE. That's easy for you to say, Claire. You work in New York all the time. You do guest spots on T.V. You have the soap. I'm just acting for health insurance these days! I'm sorry. I don't know where that came from.

(TOM enters holding his shoes in one hand and a cake box in the other.)

TOM. Hi-lo.

CLAIRE. Hello darling, come on up.

CHARLOTTE. I'm sorry, Claire.

CLAIRE. Hello darling. You remember Charlotte.

TOM. Of course…We ran into Carolyn and Wally. Malcolm's getting some pictures of the cliffs. They'll be up in a minute. Here's the cake.

CLAIRE. Oh, you're a love. What do I owe you?

TOM. Stop it, it's my gift to Carolyn.

CHARLOTTE. Oh, for Carolyn's birthday – how great. I should have…why didn't I remember it was her birthday? You should have told me, I would have gotten her something.

CLAIRE. Don't be absurd, Charlotte. Just having you here is gift enough.

TOM. The little boy's room, you'll excuse me. I'll put the cake in the kitchen.

CLAIRE. The little boy's room – you are too funny.

(TOM exits.)

CHARLOTTE. He doesn't know who I am. It would have been ridiculous to write him for an audition. Although, you never know…

CLAIRE. I'm sorry, darling, what were you talking about? I wasn't listening.

CHARLOTTE. Oh, nothing.

(aside) You never know if someone might drop out… get a movie…a parent die…I'll just hint around that I'm available – just in case someone…whoever is

playing Paulina…Oh, it's a long shot. I'm such a fool. He'll think me such a fool. I don't care, I'm desperate! Desperate for work.

What time does Bernard arrive? I would have driven him out, but you said he was coming by train.

CLAIRE. That brother of mine. He likes to take the train. He'll probably drop his things off at the house before he comes by. Listen to me, after all these years, I still call it "the house." I offered to have Wally pick him up at the station, but he likes the walk he says. Crazy brother.

(**TOM** *enters.*)

TOM. Did I hear you talking about Bernard? Is he coming out?

CLAIRE. Didn't I tell you? I'm…I must be getting early Alzheimer's. I didn't tell Charlotte that you and Malcolm were coming and didn't tell you and Malcolm that Bernard was coming. What's going on with me?

TOM. Maybe it's a problem with the writing.

(*Hold.*)

Is he still teaching?

CLAIRE. Bernard? Of course.

CHARLOTTE. And writing.

CLAIRE. I suppose. Not that…Well, he's never had much luck getting those plays of his produced. In a way, he's never really found his voice. Those…I don't know what you'd call them. Comedies? So he teaches. And some of his…Yoo hoo, Malcolm, come up when you're ready. Look at him, taking pictures of the cliffs. I love that man of yours. Some of his students – Bernard's – are doing quite well I hear, so he must be doing something right, even if he can't…It's a gift, playwriting. Wally was telling me…Carey, I think, or Peter something –

(**WALLY** *enters barefoot.*)

WALLY. Corey. Peterson. *(to* **TOM**, *handing him a set of keys)* Malcolm asked if you would hold onto the car keys.

TOM. Oh, fine.

CLAIRE. Hello sweetheart. Did you enjoy your walk?

WALLY. Corey Peterson and Sarah Goldstein. They both studied with Uncle Bernard.

(MALCOLM enters.)

MALCOLM. Really? We just saw his new play – Corey Peterson. I'm getting the sand out of my shoes. It was excellent.

CLAIRE. Malcolm, darling.

TOM. *Smart Life.*

MALCOLM. *Smart Life.* Beautiful title. A twenty-something gay man in an unhappy relationship…

TOM. The young gay scene.

MALCOLM. In some ways what it was for us. More "out" of course. But some of the same…hedonism. The clubs, the drugs, the pickups. There was that when we were younger.

CLAIRE. Not for you, darling. Weren't you a bit of a boy scout?

MALCOLM. Well, yes but…But a very probing play, I thought. And Tom's been –

TOM. Yes, I've just read this play by Sarah Goldstein. She studied with Bernard – that's interesting. Wonderful young writer. They asked me to take a look at it up at –

CHARLOTTE. Anything in it for me?

CLAIRE. Well he must be doing something right, Bernard. Either that or they're just extremely talented.

CHARLOTTE. Theatre talk, theatre talk, theatre talk, theatre talk, theatre talk! Oh my God! I can't take it any more! I'm going for a stroll down the beach. Just a short one. Lunch will be ready soon, won't it?

WALLY. Carolyn's in right now putting a salad together.

CHARLOTTE. Will there be more than just a salad? I'm starving. I'm joking, a salad will be fine, will be plenty.

(CHARLOTTE exits.)

TOM. You know…I bet there is no Carolyn – or at least she won't appear in the play.

(Hold.)

Who is she again? A friend from Julliard?

CLAIRE. Charlotte, yes. She always played the clown. You've met her a couple of times at opening nights.

TOM. She seems like someone it would be difficult to forget. No matter how hard one tried.

CLAIRE. *(chuckling)* Oh, be nice. I need to make a phone call. I'll be back in a mo. You boys entertain yourselves. Does anyone want a glass of wine?

WALLY. I'll wait for lunch.

CLAIRE. Tom? I know you don't drink, Malcolm.

TOM. I'll wait for lunch.

CLAIRE. If you change your mind…Wally, you'll…

WALLY. Yes, mother.

(CLAIRE exits.)

MALCOLM. There's been some erosion on the cliffs.

TOM. I wonder if that means something about us? Erosion. Probably not.

WALLY. So are you getting all geared up to work with Mom?

TOM. Oh, yes. I've wanted her to do this part for several years. And she's wanted me to stage it for her. It's just been a matter of us all being available at the same time…Oh, that's who that is. Charlotte, of course. Fitzmaurice. I didn't put the name together with the… person. How funny.

WALLY. What?

TOM. Oh, nothing.

MALCOLM. Boy, those cliffs are just magnificent. But there's been some erosion since we were last out. Have you noticed that, Wally?

TOM. Are you planning on staying out in L.A?

WALLY. I don't know – at least for now.

MALCOLM. The coast is beautiful out there.

WALLY. Believe it or not, I kind of like Los Angeles.

TOM. *(jovially)* You're crazy.

WALLY. I've thought of coming back since Mark died. I don't have many friends…a few come out for pilot season. I actually put a piece together with some of them – a really interesting –

TOM. You have the series. What are you doing on it?

MALCOLM. Writing, yes?

WALLY. If you can call it that. I mean it's fine – not what I want to do. But the pay is so good.

TOM. Stash away some dough.

WALLY. I'd rather be…I don't even know –

MALCOLM. Directing, yes?

WALLY. I mean on the show – yeah – I don't know. But the money…

TOM. Go for the money.

WALLY. But it's T.V.

TOM. So the fuck what?

MALCOLM. Don't tell him that. *(to himself)* Robert.

TOM. What?

MALCOLM. Robert. I just thought of him.

TOM. Oh.

WALLY. Adam, the lead writer – who's really the producer – I mean it's his show – completely…writing – everything. It's so funny. We basically have script meetings, develop ideas, assign ourselves episodes – he doesn't even attend most of these – he works at home. And then we write our scripts, and at the last minute he rewrites every one – I mean totally.

MALCOLM. Oh, gee.

WALLY. Pulls it out of his ass. Our names are on it…I hardly write a word. If I could just…I don't know –

MALCOLM. Are you seeing anyone?

WALLY. I met someone out there – an actor (of course). I don't know how serious it is. It's not serious. I think of my father…

MALCOLM. *(to himself)* Robert.

WALLY. Excuse me for a moment, gents. I'm going to go in see if my sister needs any help getting lunch together. Carolyn. Her own birthday and she's fixing lunch. If that isn't my mother, I don't know what is. Don't tell her I said that.

(WALLY exits.)

MALCOLM. He's so unhappy. *(after a pause)* Do you like the place we're staying at?

TOM. Sure, it's fine.

MALCOLM. Because you didn't say anything about it.

TOM. I would rather be at *The Wavecrest*. This one is a bit rustic for my taste.

MALCOLM. Well there were no rooms available there. Everything was so last minute. I think the place we're staying at is very nice, very charming.

TOM. That woman, Charlotte. Claire's classmate from Julliard. They were going to bring her in to read for Paulina and Claire asked that we not see her. Why would Claire –

MALCOLM. I've always wanted to have some property out here.

(WALLY enters.)

WALLY. She's fine – Carolyn, she doesn't need any help. I could have stayed in there and just kept her company, but she's kind of in her own world when she's putting a meal together.

CHARLOTTE. I'm back. I didn't walk very far. It's so beautiful along the shore. It's sunny but not too hot. Just right.

WALLY. Lunch should be ready soon, Charlotte.

CHARLOTTE. Are you excited about going into rehearsal with Claire?

TOM. Oh, of course.

CHARLOTTE. You haven't worked together for how long? It's been a long time, hasn't it?

TOM. Fifteen years. *(to himself)* Yes, Robert.

CHARLOTTE. It's such an unbelievable play. Well they all are, aren't they?

TOM. Oh yes.

CHARLOTTE. Just know I'm available. *(pause)* I mean, I'm sure you're all cast. But if there should be any changes, I'd love to work with you. I've always thought so highly of your work.

(aside) Why do I behave like this? Have I no dignity? No, I don't.

And you're a photographer, Malcolm?

MALCOLM. As a hobby.

CHARLOTTE. What do you do in real life?

MALCOLM. I'm a set designer.

CHARLOTTE. You are? How thrilling. Do you and Tom ever work together?

MALCOLM. Frequently.

CHARLOTTE. *(aside)* I'm so stupid. Why don't I know these things? I'm a total wreck.

WALLY. Malcolm did the sets for *Syncopation*. Didn't you and Mom see the show together?

CHARLOTTE. Oh, of course. Claire is a Tony voter. I tag along for the free tickets. I'm a terrible freeloader. What a great musical! So much fun. And the sets were spectacular!

(aside) Why don't I just get down on my knees and kiss their rings.

(CLAIRE enters.)

CLAIRE. Carolyn says luncheon will be ready shortly. She's so funny. I offered to help with the Nícoise. She wouldn't hear of it. But soon we'll have lunch out here on the deck and look out at a beautiful sea. I've made my important phone call. Who was it to? Oh, does it matter? And soon…I wonder where Bernard is? I wonder if he stopped to do some bird watching. You know he watches birds. He'll get here. Yes, we'll all sit down to a lovely lunch together and celebrate Carolyn's birthday.

PASSALUS. It's kind of you to have me.

CLAIRE. Carolyn couldn't stop talking about you, I thought I must meet this Mrs. Simmons. She's been talking about living out here year-long, Carolyn – heading the local library. Of course she's spent summers here since she was a child – as my brother and I did.

PASSALUS. Your daughter takes her duties as a librarian quite seriously.

CLAIRE. For what it's worth. Of course, it's a new library – the one out here – and almost majestic – at least in comparison to the old one, which was literally a one room shack. Carolyn is absolutely enamored of it.

PASSALUS. And yet she tells me she is interviewing for a small position at the…is it the Performing Arts Library?

CLAIRE. In the city, yes. And I take full credit for that. I've done a number of benefit readings for the library and become quite friendly with members of the administration. I believe it's certain that she will be working there shortly. It will be nice to keep her close by.

Carolyn tells me you were an actress.

PASSALUS. Oh, yes…quite some time ago. In England – never here in America. After my husband Richard's death I decided to remain in the States. It was quite exciting to learn that you were Carolyn's mother. You have given me many memorable evenings in the theatre.

CLAIRE. How nice of you. I don't trust you. That last was said to herself.

(**CHARLOTTE** *enters.*)

CHARLOTTE. Oh, I'm sorry. I didn't know you had company.

CLAIRE. Charlotte, please come barge on in, I'm teasing. This is Mrs. Simmons. A new friend of Carolyn's.

PASSALUS. Charlotte Fitzmaurice. How nice to make your acquaintance. I've had the pleasure of seeing you perform on a number of occasions and so admire your work.

CLAIRE. How surprising. Charlotte rarely performs in New York.

PASSALUS. Yes, but I do a good deal of traveling. Touring the Peloponnese. The Olympian Gods who were of course by then a mere abstraction and now the God of Israel just as abstract sends me back to Earth. I in life who covered better actors, Nikeratos, Theodorous, Thettalos – a mere swing or silent player to them and the misery, the bitterness, the days watching from the side from what you call the wings the back of the house in Hell for two millennia now I've festered a fabled place of torment, sentenced there to change my shape in perpetuity he sends me back with the power of transformation.

GOD. Change your shape, change your voice. At will.

PASSALUS. At will, he says. How nice. And I, what's in it for me? Why should I run this errand? What errand you ask?

GOD. There is a young woman, Carolyn.

PASSALUS. I say no more, I let you wonder why, why I come for her. I only say I do. And for this errand that he sends me back I bargain. What's in it for me?

GOD. What do you desire?

PASSALUS. You have to ask? You to whom all hearts are open, all desires known, pardon my flippancy Lord, but as we speak freely…

GOD. Indeed. But as this is a play, a passing fiction, and your thoughts be known they must be spoke aloud. You kid with me, I kid with you.

PASSALUS. Oblivion. Annihilation of the soul. Let nothing remain. I take you at your word.

GOD. All are reduced to atoms.

PASSALUS. Ultimately, yes. And smaller still. But as we barter, please, remit on receipt.

GOD. It is as you say. You go back now to the planet, do my handiwork, succeed, you will be vaporized.

PASSALUS. Scatter me far. I wish never to reconstitute.

GOD. It is as you wish.

PASSALUS. Then I am God's servant: in you is perfect freedom. Hurl me back.

GOD. Touch her only. You are only for her, for Carolyn. With no other life may you tamper. You do the bargain is null.

PASSALUS. It is as you say. How shall I go, in what guise? I need survey the scene before I bustle in the world. And now I sit here on a warm Sunday afternoon in conversation a British matron the part I create. It seems we are often in the same city at the same time. And to my good fortune. I have an especially fond memory of your Mrs. Gibbs. Heart I have I have no memory of when living strange.

CHARLOTTE. Oh, well, wow. Thank you, that's very kind of you. *(aside)* I'm flustered. No one ever pays me compliments.

I ran into Wally, Tom, and Malcolm in town. Time means nothing, does it, no, span of days, chronology. They were about to drive out to the point. They should be here any time now.

PASSALUS. *(Crouching on the ground. Upset.)* How can this be happening to me?

BERNARD. Oh, excuse me, are you all right?

PASSALUS. *(turning around)* What? Oh yes.

BERNARD. I didn't mean to surprise you. I just…

PASSALUS. *(rising)* Oh, no. Oh no! with my mask dropped, he finds me as I am, crouched here having…no don't say it, let it unfold. I'm fine – I was just – we wore masks back then, as we assumed our characters. I have dropped mine, having seen him the night before at his sister's home. He finds me as I am.

BERNARD. Gee, you're the first person I've ever encountered up here. It's so overgrown, no one ever stumbles…finds their way to this spot.

PASSALUS. Really? What the hell do I – Yeah it's I just really kind of a –

BERNARD. This was formerly the grounds of a military base – during World War II.

PASSALUS. Oh, really?

BERNARD. Yes. I've known this place since I was a child. My father and I discovered it. It's one of the best views of the ocean around here.

PASSALUS. I see.

BERNARD. *(offering his hand)* I'm Bernard.

PASSALUS. *(shaking **BERNARD**'s hand)* Passalus. I can't believe I used my real name. Oh shut up, what's the big deal, he's never heard of you.

BERNARD. Passalus?

PASSALUS. It's Greek. For god's sake it not like he's going to go online and find your press clippings from Epidaurus. *(Crouching in the ground. Upset.)* What's this? What's this? This was not supposed to happen. He's ludicrous. How can I have any feeling for him? How can I have feelings for anyone? I never did and now… How can this be happening to me?

BERNARD. Oh, excuse me, are you all right?

PASSALUS. *(turning around)* What? Oh yes.

BERNARD. I didn't mean to surprise you. I just…

PASSALUS. *(rising)* Oh no, I'm fine – I was just…

BERNARD. You're the first person I've ever encountered up here.

PASSALUS. You've seen me, but don't know it. How could you in the form of an English matron? But I sat across from you and heard you speak, speak of birds, of plays, heard your sister run wheels around you, mocking you.

CLAIRE. Bernard, you finally found your way here. I thought we'd never see you. You missed lunch. Carolyn was disappointed. You'll stay for dinner. Wally is cooking.

BERNARD. I'm sorry. I just had an idea about some writing and wanted to get it down on paper.

CLAIRE. You and those plays of yours. Come meet Mrs. Simmons.

CHARLOTTE. It's true, there is no chronology. What a marvelous gift you brought, Bernard, that old record. Carolyn was so touched. Ralph Richardson reading Blake.

CLAIRE. Mrs. Simmons, this is my brother, Bernard.

PASSALUS. *(offering hand to* **BERNARD***)* Constance. How do you do?

BERNARD. *(accepting the offered hand)* Pleased to make your acquaintance. Bernard.

PASSALUS. *(shaking* **BERNARD's** *hand)* Passalus.

BERNARD. You've been to the East End before, I guess.

PASSALUS. No, this is actually my first time out here. I arrived yesterday.

BERNARD. And you found this spot. That's amazing.

PASSALUS. I've been here for about a month now. I rent a cottage just outside of town.

CLAIRE. Carolyn has been showing Mrs. Simmons around. There's something about her I don't trust.

PASSALUS. I took the train out, and so I am without an automobile.

BERNARD. It's a beautiful ride, isn't it?

PASSALUS. I beg your pardon?

BERNARD. The train.

PASSALUS. The train, oh yes it was lovely.

BERNARD. Did you notice as you neared———————

———————————————————————————

———————————————————————

———————

PASSALUS. And he spoke of birds you spoke of birds then you spoke of plays and birds whales and dolphins of things you love, stars ink-black nights as swirls of swirling stars, Kepler's laws (Oh, my goodness!) flying in the face of Ptolemy, oh Bernard if you could see the skies I have seen Epheos, Samos, Halikarnassos, Miletos – the night skies before electric light, and Ospreys (Ospreys?) how the gulls try to make them drop their prey. (Is that right?) You went on, the poetry of your thoughts, how the others are deaf to it I do not know, the flickering tea lights and the hiss of mosquitoes zapped in that strange contraption. None of them listened as I but I as Charlotte listens yes to you as much as she can to you, struck too by your poetry, she always yes I expect, but she has always been distracted by Claire's spotlight, her attention wavers. And I followed you about the deck, first with my eyes, then with my thoughts, as you spoke, and they indulged you, and then I could not resist, I had to ask you questions The Great Gray Owl? Why, no I –

BERNARD. *Strix Nebulosa.*

PASSALUS. Its concave face a radar disk you told me standing beside you so close you see an old lady I shouldn't say old in her seventies that I am you spilled your drink on my dress you were so excited talking about –

BERNARD. St. John Ervine.

PASSALUS. St. John…?

BERNARD. Irish playwright. Early to mid Twentieth –

PASSALUS. Ervine, why yes of course flipping through my files fast fast hurryhurryhurry there oh ah *The First Mrs. Fraser.*

BERNARD. Exactly, it's a wonderful piece. And his treatise *How to Write A Play*.

PASSALUS. *How to Write a Play* an obscure book about where the hell did you find no more I can say, what's this, what's this? It's only water, please, it will dry, I promise you. I'll never forget Philanthos a rookie toasting Lamprias after Lamprias was crowned finally! at the Dionysia accidentally dropping a sausage on Menekrates' purple cloak livid don't worry it will come out with water and he burst into tears he was a talented kid whatever happened to him succumbed to drink I think he did and died in Corinth his Aegystus was sublime I don't drive and I've been staying rather close to the beach just outside of town. But Carolyn has very kindly offered to drive me out to Springs I believe it's called.

CHARLOTTE. Oh, it's very interesting. The Jackson Pollack house. Bernard, you took me –

CLAIRE. Bernard took Carolyn and Wally there, when they were younger.

WALLY. Lots of times, it's great. Mark dead a year now what am I doing in Los Angeles? Getting away from my mother is what I'm doing. The work we did out there on Chapters. Beautiful work, Wally. Thanks Charlotte – that means a lot. My mother "The stage, the stage," and sweetie pie your work – so outré. Oh please don't let me shoot my brains out at the end of Act 4.

MALCOLM. Everything was delicious, Wally.

PASSALUS. Quite delicious.

TOM. I didn't realize you were such a cook.

WALLY. Carolyn is putting the coffee on. Mark, did you die too slowly? Did it take too long the last walk along the shore in Santa Monica, the fog by the Ferris Wheel. Your drinking – that didn't help. Tom and Malcolm and all of Tom's infidelities. We sat down in the sand and watched the waves the Pacific and now I'm here the Atlantic.

PASSALUS. Tune out his voice. Wally. No – his thoughts for his dead lover. I am for Carolyn.

CLAIRE. Mrs. Simmons is quite the voracious reader. She's become quite friendly with Carolyn.

PASSALUS. Constance, please. For Carolyn only. I am not to tinker with to tamper with no other other lives.

WALLY. Oh, at the Library.

CLAIRE. Bernard, you look as though you're not with us.

BERNARD. No, I'm just thinking about something. For the play.

CLAIRE. The play. The play. Those plays that he writes. They start here, they go there. You practically need a map to follow them.

PASSALUS. I was looking at a map and just wondered where this road led to. Conversation of course. He and I.

BERNARD. If you'd like, I'd be happy to show you around. There are some wonderful trails in the dunes at Napeague. Hardly anyone goes out there – and the bay there is beautiful. If you like birds…do you…are you interested in –

PASSALUS. His arms, the hair on his arms. Um…yes, I do. I heard there are even…Ospreys.

BERNARD. Oh, yes you must see the we discussed going out on the walk back to the highway the Osprey nests did I talk too shoot I'm always after talking walking a bit further much on the bluff, taking in the view of the ocean. Coffee with half and half.

PASSALUS. Thank you very much.

BERNARD. Coffee isn't much without half and half.

(**PASSALUS** *chuckles with delight.*)

And you don't take sugar, right?

PASSALUS. Nope.

BERNARD. Sweet roll?

PASSALUS. *(after a split-second of resistance)* Sure.

BERNARD. Great, 'cause I got two.

PASSALUS. *(smiling)* When was the last time I was happy? Daeas. Daeas my dear, when first we met.

BERNARD. Patrick died…well, it's sixteen years now.

PASSALUS. Were you together long?

BERNARD. Look right there. That's an Osprey. Just like I said, with a fish in his talons. And see, look look look, here come the gulls –

PASSALUS. Oh yes!

BERNARD. See them how the gulls – mobbing him, trying to make him drop it.

PASSALUS. Oh, my goodness! I think of you to this day. Daeas. Dancer in the chorus. I did have feelings once, didn't I. That's amazing!

BERNARD. Just four years together, Patrick and I. Though it seemed longer than that.

PASSALUS. No one since then?

BERNARD. Dating, oh, well, yes, yes. But Patrick…we were both…It was a difficult, very difficult…

PASSALUS. My yelling at you Daeas that last night in my apartment how much I hated you for ending it, and I never had a chance to say how sorry I was for saying that. Monster that I am.

BERNARD. He could be a monster, Patrick. We weren't well suited. Maybe we were… He was angry. AIDS made him angrier. We would have split up, but then he got sick. Nursing him at home. Stays in the hospital. All before the cocktail. The lesions, the wasting. It went on he suffered so long. And his parents. Mississippi. They didn't know he was gay until he got sick. Or so they said. They refused to see him, then they refused to accept the body. I had him cremated. A cousin (of his) in Arizona asked for the ashes. I sent them to her. And after he was gone as years passed I loved him again – for how he was when we first met and then for knowing who he really was. I didn't love him any less for that. Not that I could have stayed with him…He was a sad man.

And there you can see his mate with the chicks – dropping off the fish.

PASSALUS. Beautiful. Daeas. When first we met, the chorus of Ezekiel's *Exagōgē*, how beautiful I thought you were handsome boyish a year older than me. Making out madly on the street, mashing our tongues together. You're gone. To Heaven I hope. And I'm two millennia away. Time a constant present.

BERNARD. My sister is having a barbecue tomorrow night. I wonder if you'd like to come by. It will be a bunch of theatre people. They'll be a lot of talk about the theatre. Not plays, they don't often talk about plays, sometimes Tom does a friend of my sister – they talk about theatre.

He tells me he was an actor.

PASSALUS. Quite a long time ago. A very long time.

BERNARD. I don't know if you've spent much time around theatre people. They'll be a lot of talk about theatre.

PASSALUS. Do I tell him I was an actor? I was an actor. Don't tell him that. I was an actor. Don't tell him that. He'll ask me what I do now. I was an actor. Quite a long time ago. A very long time. I was not particularly –

BERNARD. You gave it up?

PASSALUS. Sort of. I still I well I tell him I'm in – I don't know what I'll tell him. That I…work with people and it involves…playacting, performing…in an odd sort of way. Great write yourself out of that one what…doesn't everyone kind of…office! think fast for god's sake an… administrative assistant a secretary a sort of at a…law firm that sounds generic enough. The attorneys I work for – talk about drama! Do I accept the invitation? How can I? Claire has invited me as Mrs. Simmons, and I've agreed to attend. But if I decline…Passalus.

CLAIRE. How nice to meet you. What an odd name. I don't trust him anymore than I trust that Simmons woman. Where is she by the way? No, Carolyn tells me she's getting here on her own steam this evening, Mrs. Simmons. Malcolm, you and those cliffs – look at him with his camera! Passalus what an odd name Greek how interesting my Hecuba I once played Hecuba –

PASSALUS. Oh this stupid woman, if she knew how many actors talked about their Hecuba.

CLAIRE. I have a second sense of people. People I don't trust. Of course I was much too young for the part there's something about him I don't trust there was James of course, oh Bernard – the many men you've dated since Patrick. Our Bernard and the many many men.

BERNARD. Jimmy.

CLAIRE. Jimmy yes of course you called him. Jimmy – James – whatever. Who else was there? There was Peter, Peter and Jerry, Tom and Huck, Tom and Jerry I'm teasing darling. The list goes on and on. So you met my brother at the "spot" as Bernard calls it. It was his and my father's "spot." Their special place. I was there once. All that overgrown muddy ground. And the insects. Once was quite enough.

MALCOLM. Because you like power.

TOM. Stop it.

MALCOLM. Boys from the chorus. You don't think there's a reason you run after –

TOM. Maybe it has something to do with the fact that they're good looking.

MALCOLM. Does it?

TOM. Ballet class in the gymnasium sophomore year the smell of sweat and scrotum. Good looking.

MALCOLM. As though I'm not is what I'm thinking.

TOM. I've never really found you attractive. Your body disgusts me.

MALCOLM. There are things you can't take back, Tom. Your body disgusts me he says.

TOM. I'm sorry. It's me, not you, your body is fine. It's me, the problem is me. Then months of him sleeping on the couch after that to punish me.

MALCOLM. You think there isn't a power imbalance? Crawling back into the bed after months on the couch

I feel the fool. A kid in the chorus – a famous director you think he's not going to be star struck. Slept with him. He slept with him and how many others? You think people don't know, that they don't talk?

TOM. Behind these eyes I'm dead what's that from? *The Entertainer* – Olivier – of course.

MALCOLM. Do you know what people think about you, Tom? Say about you? About us?

TOM. *The Entertainer.* How the hell did I remember that? We've always had an understanding. I can't help myself. Say that to him: Malcolm, I can't help myself and it's true. It's like a slide, a spiral slide and I'm grabbing hold to the sides but slipping.

MALCOLM. You had an understanding I didn't. The pornography I use while he's at his office. Boys from the chorus or studs he picks up at the gym.

TOM. When we met first what have I become? Have I no conscience? Yes no. Please, he'll leave me if it doesn't stop.

MALCOLM. Stop the design due on the 16th no more porno. Others think it's fine and the hook ups on line they do I hear about I'd never shame sham marriage make do.

PASSALUS. Their voices tune out and the memories their memories like open books. I'm torn between life and death. Death all knowing walking on the Earth. The suffering I suffered this way too – not only Malcolm but Tom's, Malcolm's withdrawals. No stop only. I only come for Carolyn to help to free.

I beg your pardon. The walk was longer than I thought.

CLAIRE. Oh, Mrs. Simmons. Carolyn will be so happy you're here.

CHARLOTTE. Carolyn will never appear though she exists unless one of us plays her.

CLAIRE. You remember Tom. Where has Malcolm gone?

PASSALUS. Ah, yes. Charmed to see you again.

CHARLOTTE. There is no chronology. Tom and Malcolm were here, we all were here the afternoon Mrs. Simmons first came here. And the look in her eyes when Bernard together on the deck.

CLAIRE. Charlotte, quick, look. If I didn't know any better I'd think that Carolyn's Mrs. Simmons is taken with my brother. Look at her hanging on his every word.

CHARLOTTE. Birds, the planetary ellipses, and how he hopes some day to weave them into a play the *How to Write a Play* by and Claire you've always despised your brother with the utmost politeness. Why I think you're right, Claire, she does seem Bernard how it was from when we were young a poetry to you. Always. That day in my striped dress and Wally.

CLAIRE. I don't know how to break it to her. I don't know how to tell you this, Mrs. Simmons (can you imagine my saying this), you are not my brother's type inner monologue my brother's type likes men not women not women in their seventies despite how they might find rapture in his everything he says inner monologue over birds and beasts and what have you Bernard stop monopolizing poor Mrs. Simmons. I'm afraid you'll bore her terribly.

PASSALUS. Not in the least I find this————

CLAIRE. I've got news for you dear my dear lady that first night they met and now she shows up late where is that Passalus? I'm sorry Mrs. –

PASSALUS. Constance please call me.

CLAIRE. Bernard's gentleman friend…where has he gone off to?

PASSALUS. Oh yes, the gentleman I met at the front of the house okay honey let's start acting now. Passalus, I believe he said.

TOM. Yes, that's him about time I started talking too many thoughts to myself Malcolm and I tomorrow he'll leave me if I'm not…

BERNARD. Hello Constance.

PASSALUS. Good evening Bernard.

TOM. Malcolm and Bernard were going to show him the cliffs.

BERNARD. There are Cliff Swallows I wanted him to see and Malcolm wanted to point out the erosion on the bluffs.

CLAIRE. Wanted who to see?

BERNARD. Passalus.

CLAIRE. Oh yes look Charlotte look just as she was the last time she was here looking at Bernard like a puppy in love. As you yourself have looked at Bernard haven't you Charlotte I must never dare say that to her.

WALLY. Mother what are you gawking at?

CLAIRE. I'm just pointing out to Charlotte (who will never have the career that I have will she no no no no no) that your uncle has found an admirer.

WALLY. Mother, you're being cruel.

CHARLOTTE. Yes, Claire, yes the things I might never say to you. How cruel you can be god knows what you say behind my back.

PASSALUS. Well that's one thing about reading other people's thoughts you know I'm half tempted to expose that woman to the others their inner voices tamper I must not for Carolyn only. Malcolm is back.

MALCOLM. I never noticed Bernard those swallows. Those are Cliff Swallows?

BERNARD. Cliff Swallows or Cave Swallows. I'm ashamed to say I don't know.

CLAIRE. What's happened to Bernard's gentleman friend?

MALCOLM. He wanted to stay a little longer looking at cliffs I was pointing out the cliffs and how over the years———

PASSALUS. The long years that he and Tom have come out here and the thoughts racing through his mind right at this minute. Will he just grab the car keys, storm out of here and leave that fucker Tom to his own devices.

You want to don't you don't you Malcolm. But should you?

You were directed many times by your husband, I believe.

WALLY. My father.

TOM. Robert. To myself. What did I do to you? But you never knew, nothing ever came of it.

MALCOLM. Robert. Tom will never be Robert. He'll never be thought of as Robert was.

WALLY. Mother, please – you never speak with me about. She never speaks with me about my father. Never. My ideal. T.V.? Six when he. His death. And I don't even remember.

CLAIRE. It was a true partnership, Robert and I. That Passalus, one minute he's here, Mrs. Simmons – Constance – pardon me – the next minute he's gone.

PASSALUS. Yes, he does seem to come and go. But you were saying. And the evening presses on, my exiting as one then entering as the other on and on the farce of it the close calls played so many times why play it again?

CLAIRE. We met through Tom – Robert and I. He was going to leave me but then he got ill. He and Tom were both aspiring directors. He never let me get away with anything on the stage. I had always to be truthful for him. Our work together so meaningful, though Carolyn and Wally meant more to him than anything. Wally is Tom's son, but only Robert and I knew it. Now only I know it. Robert knew. He loved Wally even though. And Tom he loved he knew why I so much. Tom he got to Robert through me I've let him think. My humanity. No, it was I got to Robert through Tom and Robert knew it and he protected Tom and my soul is burning. Poor Tom so stupid. That's why I let him direct me I suppose because I know I can get what I want he'll help me.

PASSALUS. But he'll never get the truth out of you as Robert did. So in a way you and he Tom and you are collaborators as well.

CLAIRE. Yes we are.

PASSALUS. He can't help you as your husband did, but he can help you.

CLAIRE. What's that you say?

PASSALUS. Just my sense from what you said how close you and your husband worked. And that Tom – Tom will never –

Your sister is an actress.

BERNARD. Oh, both she and Charlotte.

PASSALUS. No, no, I mean your sister is an *actress*! At every moment – even when she's asking someone to pass the butter.

CLAIRE. Pass the butter, will you darling.

CHARLOTTE. How are you holding up, champ?

WALLY. Fine.

CHARLOTTE. Your uncle actually has a date this evening. I loved Mark. Your father would be very proud of you.

PASSALUS. Perhaps then you should talk to him, Charlotte, to Wally. I'm saying this from the pictures in your head the words in your thoughts. If that's what you think.

CHARLOTTE. It's killing him out there. Not the place. Running to me I had on that blue striped dress blowing in the breeze the Summer air the sea air and your pail and shovel your little bathing trunks. Go and play with Wally will you Charlotte. Go to Aunt Charlotte, Wally. Please Claire, I'm not his aunt. Look Aunt Charlotte, look, the shells. Oh, please be happy Wally.

PASSALUS. Charlotte how much longer will you...

CHARLOTTE. It's just that Claire...they both want to get away, don't they Carolyn and.

PASSALUS. You want to get away from her too, don't you?

CHARLOTTE. I was out – I had a little blink and you'll miss me part in a movie – in Los Angeles. A famous director. I brushed a spider off his shoulder. He yelled at one of the extras so badly. And Wally did this wonderful piece with actors out there, he gave them these improvisations based on –

WALLY. We're basing them on the stories and short novels.

CHARLOTTE. *(to* **WALLY***)* Oh, really? *(to* **PASSALUS***)* Of Chekhov – it was very ambitious. Not all of it worked. *Chapters* he called it. *Chapters.* In this dark little theatre. It was beautiful. *(to* **WALLY***)* It's beautiful. *(to* **PASSALUS***)* It was beautiful.

PASSALUS. Tell him Charlotte, free him, I can't do it.

CHARLOTTE. Friends of his, these actors, were out for pilot season working with him. It's a shame, most of them are in New York. But he's hoping some of them will be heading back out again.

PASSALUS. Perhaps you should tell him.

BERNARD. Oh, there you are, I was wondering. Looking at the cliffs?

PASSALUS. For a moment, then I was looking at the stars.

CHARLOTTE. Wally, you know those –

PASSALUS. Go 'head, Charlotte tell him. He ran to you that Summer day with his pail and shovel and hugs you his wet hair and face against your dress, and all the winter holidays in the city, their brownstone on the Upper West Side. He's six years old, Aunt Charlotte, Aunt Charlotte, send him off, free yourself after all these years.

CHARLOTTE. If I could I never married my son my heart is filled with love and rage. Go, Wally, while you can –

PASSALUS. Perhaps you should *tell him Charlotte.*

CHARLOTTE. *(to* **WALLY***)* Feel like stretching your legs?

WALLY. Sure, let's take a walk.

CLAIRE. Where are you two going?

CHARLOTTE. Just taking a walk.

CLAIRE. Something is not right tonight. I feel something. Something is loosening. It could bring this house down I've worked for so many years to build up. The phone call today. No. No. *(to* **TOM** *and* **MALCOLM***)* What are you boys thinking about? Where is that, now they're both gone that Passalus and Mrs. Simmons.

Will someone nail them down! In and out the two of them. What are you thinking about, Bernard?

BERNARD. The play, how it's proceeding.

CLAIRE. What *do* you mean?

BERNARD. In my head, the scenes, the passages. I've had this play in mind for years.

CLAIRE. Him and those plays of his. Something is wrong. I feel it. I can't hold it together.

TOM. I like Bernard's plays, I always have.

CLAIRE. You never mentioned that to me.

MALCOLM. Oh course he has you just don't listen. This is said to himself.

CLAIRE. I'm not a monster. What is Malcolm thinking?

MALCOLM. You just don't listen.

TOM. I have, I always have. Strange little, they're like strange little objects. I wouldn't know what to do with them. But I find them intriguing none-the-less.

MALCOLM. Tell him then. Tell him to tell him then. You should tell him that.

TOM. I always have.

PASSALUS. Bejeweled sky, isn't it?

BERNARD. Oh, there you are, I lost track of you.

PASSALUS. I was just inside speaking with Carolyn. For the last time. My job is done.

BERNARD. Have you had a chance to speak with my friend Passalus.

PASSALUS. I'm afraid not, and I must be going rather shortly. Inside I heard you Malcolm tell him. Free yourself. And him. Though what you are always no repair for the years. But a life together the two of you. Salvage. Carolyn is not going to take the job in the city.

BERNARD. Is that right?

PASSALUS. Tell him, Charlotte.

MALCOLM. Tell him, Tom.

TOM. Tell what?

CHARLOTTE. It's true.

WALLY. Coming from you Charlotte I'm glad – that means a lot to me it's funny the surf.

PASSALUS. The shells the pieces of – their toes in the sand. Down the beach the moon even from here their voices their thoughts.

WALLY. I suppose, but why do you mean a better actress? I've never known why you think yourself less than my mother.

CHARLOTTE. Because she is but soon I'm not caring. I think you should stay out there. His play from the stories.

WALLY. I could I'd like to. I've been to finish to stay out there I guess I could for now.

CHARLOTTE. You could – at least for now.

WALLY. I mean I could at least for now.

CHARLOTTE. Have you thought of staying out there?

WALLY. And I've thought on occasion of staying in Los Angeles – at least for now –

CHARLOTTE. And continue –

WALLY. What I do.

CHARLOTTE. Making a place for yourself.

WALLY. But make a place for myself. Create. Not just punch the clock.

CHARLOTTE. And the actors. The actors you said the ones you know are coming back out anyway.

WALLY. Some of them – maybe…but there could be others.

CHARLOTTE. There are always others.

WALLY. And there's no reason I can't go back and forth.

CHARLOTTE. There's no reason you can't go back and forth.

PASSALUS. Because a play in ellipses.

WALLY. And return when I'm…When I'm ready.

PASSALUS. In a sequence finding another way.

MALCOLM. Tell him, then.

TOM. Tell what?

CHARLOTTE. Let's head back.

MALCOLM. *(to* **PASSALUS**, *Mrs. Simmons)* Tom has always loved Bernard's plays. But, you know, Claire. He's never really said much.

PASSALUS. Perhaps he should.

MALCOLM. Yes, perhaps he should.

PASSALUS. Perhaps you should tell him to. He is after all… your partner. Surely he listens to you.

MALCOLM. It's not like I'm God. For the actor playing Malcolm plays God. Godliness or most in need of God? Let those who know say.

TOM. Two boys in the West 50's – Malcolm the mattress on the floor the sheets wet with –

MALCOLM. And now you direct the whole household.

TOM. And then the road home – two men in the dark pushing forward against the night the headlights opening the darkness before them.

MALCOLM. Two men in the dark moving through the night.

PASSALUS. Error not evil, correction not catastrophe.

MALCOLM. You should tell Bernard, how much you like his plays. I've known it for years. I've told him. But coming from you, Tom.

WALLY. It would mean a lot.

MALCOLM. It would mean a lot.

TOM. Yes. I guess it would.

PASSALUS. And so the night speeds on its way. And the graves are op'd.

I'm…ancient.

BERNARD. Oh, please.

PASSALUS. No, I mean really ancient.

BERNARD. I'm in my forties.

PASSALUS. "About" the same.

BERNARD. That's hardly ancient. Tell me a story.

PASSALUS. There once was a man who hated life.

BERNARD. Why?

PASSALUS. His dreams. His fantasies.

BERNARD. What did he want?

PASSALUS. Fame.

BERNARD. Tell me this story. But tell it differently – not as you began it.

PASSALUS. Imagine a scene. Two men on a pleasant Summer day by the shore. On a rise that looks over the sea. Passing gulls and terns.

BERNARD. As we are now. Mockingbirds, Blue Jays, Cardinals. There are waxwings in the trees behind them. Cedar Waxwings.

PASSALUS. I'm looking for a form to tell this story. Perhaps it is a play – of some type.

BERNARD. Let it be fantastical, but grounded in something you know. Painted Buntings, finches Black-capped Chickadees.

PASSALUS. Yes, you must tell a story of something you know.

BERNARD. Two men on a grassy knoll overlooking the sea. A picnic. They met at this spot a week before. They made love for the first time this afternoon.

PASSALUS. The hedge, the picture window, a sliver of the ocean. The little house by the sea. And now one of them is telling the other one a story. It is the story of himself, but he is telling it as if it were a fiction. For it is so impossible seeming, it can only be told as a fiction.

BERNARD. Keep going.

PASSALUS. These two men.

BERNARD. And the ocean below.

PASSALUS. Leave it for now and pick it up tomorrow.

BERNARD. Okay, it's tomorrow.

PASSALUS. There was once an actor who dreamed of fame, longed for it. Hungered for it.

BERNARD. Tell me more of this story.

PASSALUS. I've had this story in my head for years.

BERNARD. Would you tell it to me?

PASSALUS. It's nothing.

BERNARD. You never know, it might give me an idea for a play.

PASSALUS. I might have to sue you for plagiarism.

BERNARD. How about we split the proceeds down the middle?

PASSALUS. I don't think my story will be worth much.

BERNARD. Let me hear.

PASSALUS. Imagine, if you will, an actor – Athens. Two hundred years before the common era. He struggles for years to make himself a leading player. Believes he will become one. Believes at times he is one. Even tries his hand at tragedies and comedies – succeeds at neither. Tours the Peloponnese – small companies. Relegated – on the one occasion he makes it to the Dionysia – to a non-speaking role, an understudy to the third actor. He's watched his peers succeed one after the other – some of whom started with him in the chorus of Agathon's *Antheus*.

BERNARD. What becomes of him?

PASSALUS. Not much. As he grows older he grows bitter – bitter that life has passed him by. His end…is uneventful. Swept away in time.

BERNARD. Go on.

PASSALUS. He never knew himself, he never loved. Oh, there were affairs, one especially, painful, as youthful affairs can be. Friends who never really knew him.

BERNARD. Knew him no better than he knew himself.

PASSALUS. So that's the happy story I want to write.

BERNARD. Does it end with his death?

PASSALUS. No. This is where it gets most fantastical. Because you see it's not historical drama.

BERNARD. How old are you?

PASSALUS. I'm…ancient.

BERNARD. No, really.

PASSALUS. I'm serious.

BERNARD. More than forty?

PASSALUS. Way more.

BERNARD. Fifty?

PASSALUS. Fifty?! Do I look like I'm fifty?!

> He goes back, for God, to free a young woman trying to make a life for herself. And for his reward he insists on full eradication. His masquerade? Life in the old girl yet. He puts on the wig – so to speak – takes on the character of…an old woman, say. But…

BERNARD. But?

PASSALUS. It's preposterous. Among the characters he meets, an actress – a journey man, not a star, he pays her a compliment, coming from he knows not where – a spot a little spot on the heart an empathy as she stands in the cold shadow of her better recognized friend. And from then each one he meets…even the girl's mother…he feels for them, players in a passing show. Struggling players. And then…

BERNARD. And then? What happens then?

GOD. Your shape shifting power is stripped. You stay as you are.

PASSALUS. I did as we bargained.

GOD. No, you were meant only for Carolyn, not to mix yourself up in anyone else's life.

PASSALUS. There was no help for it. Once it started it could not be stopped.

GOD. You have only yourself to blame.

PASSALUS. You promised me oblivion.

GOD. Tell me.

PASSALUS. Each one of them, they needed a tug or a tickle. To move an inch. To shift the balance. I had to free Wally and I could only do it through Charlotte by freeing her. I could only free Malcolm by his freeing Tom. And Tom will never know the secret and what good would it do him or Wally?

GOD. Is that what you wish? An end?

PASSALUS. An end of me, yes.

GOD. Why?

PASSALUS. You know as well as I. To you my heart is open. There is no other way.

He fell in love.

BERNARD. Who? The little demon.

PASSALUS. Yes. Over many days not transcribed.

You who see all, know all, see in your mind's eye what I am, what I was, what I became, what I become. Would you return me to Hell? An eternity seeing him in my mind's eye?

GOD. You have broken the contract. You tampered in lives. I leave you in life.

PASSALUS. No. Worse than Hell.

GOD. There is no help for it.

PASSALUS. Then return me from where I was plucked. If you will not grant me oblivion, grant me eternal torment. Let my punishment distract me.

GOD. No. You will finish your days.

PASSALUS. I didn't intend it. You know why I can't stay. He can't love me. He won't love me. You know what he said.

The man of his heart, to whom he fell, confessed to the woman he masqueraded as, that he did not –

BERNARD. I do very much Mrs. Simmons –

PASSALUS. Constance.

BERNARD. Constance, yes, like him, that is. Passalus.

PASSALUS. This was said the day after to her as she prepared to leave. And there was hope in his heart.

BERNARD. But I'm a solitary creature. I can't. I can't.

PASSALUS. And it went on, all the reasons he could not.

So if you leave me here, who will have me? The age you leave me at, and all I bring to it, who will love me? No one. No one. I'm old. I'll be alone, I'll be unhappy.

GOD. You didn't have to intercede on behalf of the others.

PASSALUS. I pitied them.

GOD. Thus I pity you.

BERNARD. At the train station. I told you there'd be a train station.

PASSALUS. Hi.

BERNARD. I heard you were leaving today. I ran into Charlotte. She told me. On her way back into town. Wally left last night. Back to L.A. Tom and Malcolm the night before.

PASSALUS. Yes.

BERNARD. You're going…

PASSALUS. Into the city. I found a place to live.

BERNARD. I love taking the train. I love taking it out here and I love the ride home to the city.

PASSALUS. What are you doing here?

BERNARD. I spoke to Mrs. Simmons, to Constance. We were speaking of love. And I told her there was someone… and that I couldn't…that I hadn't since Patrick loved I thought I could rejoin the race but that I was a solitary man. I didn't think I could love again. There is no chronology.

PASSALUS. This is what he says at the train station.

You who knows all, hears all. You know what he said. That he couldn't love. More oblivion do I wish for now than ever.

BERNARD. It's the funniest thing, I was walking along the shore. I had just said goodbye to Mrs. Simmons (Constance). And an old man walked up behind me. I can't for life of me summarize our conversation, we spoke of so many things.

PASSALUS. An old man, you say?

BERNARD. And we sat on a log, watching the gulls and a family of crows pecking in the sand. He spoke to me of so many things, of two young men on another beach, one of them near death, a fog a Ferris Wheel. Of a woman, lonely but good-hearted who gropes and finds her way, livid that she forgot a young woman's birthday. Of two men in the dark returning home. And a young woman freed at last to find her own life, all of them freed finally, and that these miracles…Well, that they were that. Miracles. He sat looking quietly at the sea and I imagined someone waiting for me in the moonlight. Looking up at the stars, the vesper light, the swallows twirling around him. Cave Swallows. Cliff Swallows.

PASSALUS. *(to* **CLAIRE***)* They will all leave you, I'm afraid. Before the night is through. As must I. I bid you farewell.

(He turns from her.)

CLAIRE. Who are you? Who are you really? I have never trusted you.

(He turns back as himself. **CLAIRE** *is startled by what she sees. It's all up to the actress playing Claire – and the actor playing Passalus; for there is of course, no visual change.)*

(A small gasp.) Ah!

PASSALUS. I bid you adieu.

She will be dead of cancer in a year. The phone call in the first scene. The important call. Her doctor. Because even when there is pathos, there is not always tragedy. Those that leave her do not abandon her. And she leaves her mark. She entertained many.

BERNARD. And I knew then.

PASSALUS. Knew what?

BERNARD. Begin your dialogue at I have an apartment. Go 'head.

PASSALUS. I believe that's your line.

BERNARD. Oh, yes.

I have an apartment in the city, and this small house out here.

PASSALUS. The small house by the sea. It's a very nice house. You keep it up so well. The house.

BERNARD. And it's on a rise. I don't tell many people this, I usually say we have no view of the ocean; but you know if you're standing in the right spot, under that tree, that old tree, there is a sliver of ocean.

PASSALUS. Oh, wow. Well, the train is going to arrive any moment.

BERNARD. Go back to where you are.

(Hold.)

Go back to where you are. Where you are living. Who you are and where you are and when you are. We do sometimes get second chances and life unfolds as we had given up. But it surprises us and unfolds and this time we are ready. Go back to where you are.

PASSALUS. What?

BERNARD. Say it. Because I can love you.

PASSALUS. I got an apartment in the city. And Charlotte arranged for me to meet her agent. They agreed to give me a try and sent me out on an audition. I got the part.

BERNARD. Really, what is it?

PASSALUS. A small part in *Romeo and Juliet*.

BERNARD. What part?

PASSALUS. Peter.

BERNARD. Peter?

PASSALUS. The Nurse's servant – the Nurse's cohort.

BERNARD. I don't remember that part.

PASSALUS. That's what everybody says.

BERNARD. I'm sorry…I shouldn't have –

PASSALUS. It's alright. It's a start. It's a part. And I figure I'll use my off time to work on the little play I have in mind.

BERNARD. What play is that?

PASSALUS. The little story I told you about – about the actor in Athens.

BERNARD. Oh, the story you told me.

PASSALUS. Yes. Because I think it is a play. It could be a sketch. But I think it's a play. So…And you? When do you return to the city?

BERNARD. I told her, Mrs. Simmons, I didn't think I could love another person. Not again. Because I never successfully…I never had.

When I found out you were leaving I panicked. I don't know what I'm capable of. But I would like to try. To see you, that is.

PASSALUS. This is a play.

BERNARD. *(touching* **PASSALUS***'s heart and face)* I don't want to lose you.

PASSALUS. *(touching* **BERNARD***'s face)* There's no way you could.

BERNARD. So he went into town and took the small part in the play. And Charlotte was cast in the role of the Nurse. And in his spare time and in the dressing room when he wasn't onstage he wrote the little play of himself. And that's the play I wrote, the play you've been seeing. The little play of himself and his release from Hell into life again.

(It ends with a kiss as light fades.)

End

OTHER TITLES AVAILABLE FROM SAMUEL FRENCH

SHE STOOPS TO COMEDY

David Greenspan

Comedy / 3m, 3f / Simple Set

In *She Stoops to Comedy*, Alexandra Page, a self-involved actress, known for her portrayals of tragic heroines, disguises herself as a man in order to play Orlando opposite her girlfriend, Alison Rose, who has been cast as Rosalind in an out-of-town production of *As You Like It*. Because the role of Alexandra is played by a man, her transformation does not require the use of drag. And because the other actors in the *As You Like It* cast are friends of Alexandra and Alison – and the "disguise" so effective – Alexandra has an opportunity to not only hear what people really think of her, but to be made privy to the inner lives of her friends and colleagues. The play examines the friendships and love relationships of its seven characters, and plays with the nature of authenticity – both on and off the stage.

"80 minutes of near total delight... Sweeping away everything but the mind of the playwright and the ability of the actors, Greenspan creates a fiction that has the pleasure and pain of life, plus the extravagant possibilities of the imagination. He does it without apparatus, attitude, amplification, willed ugliness... It's just theater, pure and simple. What a relief." – *The Village Voice*

SAMUELFRENCH.COM

www.ingramcontent.com/pod-product-compliance
Lightning Source LLC
Chambersburg PA
CBHW070304010526
44108CB00039B/1856